Old Man Laughing

Old Man Laughing

Poems

ROBERT KING

GHOST ROAD PRESS

Library of Congress Cataloging-in-Publication Data.

Old Man Laughing

Ghost Road Press

ISBN 0-9789456-3-8 (Trade pbk.)

Library of Congress Control Number: 2007921495

Cover painting by Bari DeJaynes

Ghost Road Press

Denver, Colorado

ghostroadpress.com

ACKNOWLEDGMENTS

Thanks to the following publications for poems which first appeared in their pages: *Atlanta Review*: "What It's Like Now"; *The Carolina Quarterly*: "Love Along the River"; *Dalhousie Review*: "Open Spaces"; *Ellipsis*: "Shelf Life"; *The Malahat Review*: "Girl at the River"; *Many Mountains Moving*: "Loss"; *The Massachusetts Review*: "Rising Up Together"; *The Missouri Review*: "One of Those Days," "Comparisons," "From the Book of Rope," "Aunts," "Instructions"; *Open Windows 2006*: "The Moment of Snow"; *Northeast*: "First Grounds"; *Northwest Review*: "It Was Xenon," "What It Was Like Those Days"; *Poetry*: "Listening in Summer," "About Eight Minutes of Light"; *South Dakota Review*: "Driving Home, Wherever That Is"; *Sundog*: "Take-out Point"; *Sycamore Review*: "Not About Clouds."

The following poems were published in chapbooks: "Goodnights" in *Learning American* (Frank Cat Press, 1998): "Crumbs," "The Maps," "School of the Art of Wings," "Falling Asleep in Florida," "On Music" and "Naming Names" in *Naming Names* (Palanquin Press, 2001), and "Life Sciences" and "A History of Photography" in *What It Was Like* (Small Poetry Press, 2003).

Contents

OLD

What It Was Like Those Days   13

The Maps   14

West of Singapore   16

Aunts   18

A History of Photography   20

First Grounds   22

Another Memento Mori   24

Life Sciences   25

Girl At the River   26

Open Spaces   27

The School of the Art of Wings   28

Take-Out Point   29

The Singing of Bob and Charlene   30

The Moment of Snow   32

Not About Clouds   33

MAN

From the Book of Rope   38

It Was Xenon, I Think   39

The Whole Time   40

Marriage Fire   42

Playing   43

Shelf Life   44

Sadnesses   45

Marriage Two: A Day At the Beach   46

Driving Home, Wherever That Is   47

Accidentals   48

Instructions   50

Dining Alone With Everyone   51

Love Along the River   53

LAUGHING

What It's Like Now   56

Naming Names   57

Listening In Summer   59

One of Those Days   61

About Eight Minutes of Light in the Meadow   62

Comparisons   63

Goodnights   64

On Music   66

At a Table on Sutter & Leavenworth   67

Appearances   69

Rising Up Together   71

Loss   73

Faltering   75

Old Man Laughing

Partial to pine cliffs and lonely trails
an old man laughs at himself when he falters
even now after all these years
trusting the current like an unmoored boat.

—Shih-Te (Red Pine, translator)

Part One

OLD

WHAT IT WAS LIKE THOSE DAYS

Since, as a child, I was happy
as a child, I thought everyone
was happy, including the grimy man
who lived at the dump in a shack
decorated with hubcaps, broken chairs
by the door cheerfully facing out to a waste
of smoldering rubble and oily dirt,
although it was a strange kind of happiness
I knew I wouldn't ever truly know.
Even the dead, I thought then,
grinning as I biked around town,
were happy in their own dead way.
That's what it was like.

THE MAPS

On the wall of the coffee shop is a map of the world
with all the countries coffee comes from brightly colored,
and the names—Tanzania, Malawi, Tongo, Jamaica—
in white letters bobbing just offshore
on the blue-green sea.

In the bread store there must be a map of the world
showing where various wheats and barleys arise
and in the natural history museum a map of dinosaurs'
buried locations, one frequently consulted by geologists.

In the hospital, there's a map where plagues are pins
or blinking lights, and in the marriage store
a map, with local inserts, showing where your future
husband or wife now lives. There's also a map,

you should understand, in the divorce store.
In the church there's a map of the various local
manifestations of God which changes periodically
when a statue exudes red liquid or drinks milk.

In the chair store there's a map showing the location
of all the chairs in the world. This map is always
changing as people get up from a table and move them,
or someone is asked to sit down or someone arrives.

In Orlando, Florida, someone is setting up chairs
in a hotel ballroom for a convention. In Paris,
a chair unaccountably tumbles from a truck
and lands upside down beside the Seine,

a small surrealist object glowing all night.
In Ogden, Iowa, a chair sits at the kitchen table,
unmoved for two years, the dead brother's jacket
draped over it, still too heavy to be lifted up.

In the sleeping store, there's a map of everywhere
people are sleeping, which looks like any map,
a cheap reprint, though probably quite accurate,
and which closely resembles the map in the dying store.

WEST OF SINGAPORE

West of Oglalla, I-80, by the feedlot,
    I lose the public classical music
which, anyway, was getting me seasick
    with its lyrical swell and falling

and pass under the half-built bridge,
    the silent trucks, the cement mixer
soundlessly rolling its round drum,
    while I seek an AM station.

"I never had it so bad," the singer intones,
    and I punch on, finishing it myself:
"and that ain't good" or else "that's good,"
    such songs balancing the way they think.

I catch an ad on asthma, and now one
    of those head-shaking ends-of-the-news,
a man flying to England to propose,
    while the woman decides to fly to him,

not even meeting, it's reported,
    as they sit in the same waiting room
in Singapore, missing each other that little.
    Although I mainly wonder "Singapore?"

I also think that what's electric in the air
    is all our lives. Driving we escape into them
again and again, pick up the pieces of ourselves
    we've denied. The next station delivers me

unto "Love Worth Finding" where Pastor Adrian
    reminds me toleration of other religious beliefs
"fits Satan's scheme perfectly" and continues
    with another slaughter by God on the boys

of Jerusalem seduced by the girls of Moab
        as I continue west. We do not live
in such large times, although we have it good
        as well as bad. Most of us sit around with asthma

in waiting rooms in Singapore, our only loves
        continually arriving and departing barely out
of our attention. Will we look around? Most
        of the time we do not and, the other side of this hill,

the symphonic ocean waits, its frequency
        often modulating with those laborious waves,
its sweet rhythm relentless across the fields, covering,
        Like death, everything with the old same sound.

AUNTS

I remember one aunt with long red hair
who laughed, at least that one afternoon.
The other, subject to some frailty I wasn't told,
kept pillows on the phones to soften
any potential intrusion. So who's to say

I don't remember the aunt who shot
clay-pigeons from horseback in Cody's show,
grit flying up, the smock-smock of the rifle?
Or that I couldn't remember the aunt
who wrote a long Victorian novel
or the aunt who married Lot
or felt afterward, she said, as if she had?

I remember the aunt with an aureole,
the aunt with an aura, the aunt colored
like an aurora with rings on her auricles
who walked au naturel through the forests,
leaves imprinting a network of lace on her flanks.

I remember the aunt who left no diary,
the one who did, the one the diary was about.
I remember the aunt who made night,
and the aunt who put the stars to flight,
the aunt who traveled into the darkness
and the aunt who traveled with the darkness.

I remember the one who discovered gold,
the gold one who discovered death,
the dead one who discovered the light,
the light one who discovered electricity
and writing and hair and gunpowder

and I remember the aunt who brushed her shining red hair
and laughed one afternoon in the pines of the mountains
and the aunt in the city who moved gently and mysteriously
through dark rooms, none of the telephones daring to speak,
while I invented my families, darkly concocting myself.

A HISTORY OF PHOTOGRAPHY

My mother, a child in Montana, amazingly
      perches, a gray prairie distance around,
on a huge hunk of granite so wondrous
      "Anderson" painted his name on it,
and peers through one day's brightness,
      a little proud to be elevated, a little shy.

I look something like her in black and white
      on a Sunday with my father
and Montana grandfather, a wary belonging,
      an uncertain smile, though I inexplicably lean
as if the earth were shifting under my feet.
      For her grandparents, photographs were once

or twice a life, regal people almost exhausted
      with style, forced to be still a long time,
while my children collect more evidence
      of weddings, parties, than they need, all of us
different chapters in a history of photography.
      In the only other childhood picture I have,

still just as bright in Montana, she poses
      as the groom in small formal suit, top hat,
with a neighbor girl in a tiny bridal dress,
      a "Tom Thumb wedding" photographers
lugged costumes for those days of strange pretend.
      My own young albums reveal a series of uniforms

I grew into, out of, tilting in the front yard
      where the apple tree has leaves, doesn't have leaves,
and I wonder—mother gone underground—
      at how strange and strong we've all been,
told to stay until stones themselves
      are worn blank of anyone's name,

and how we stand there obediently
	near marvels or in costume in the glare
and trying, usually successfully, to "be at least
	halfway happy about it" as my mother would have
coached, straightening her own shoulders
	as father took another picture of his son.

FIRST GROUNDS

This afternoon, over our heads in history
        down on our knees in an old pit-house,
we seem to be praying to the earth, slicing

years into centimeters with sharpened trowels
        in Depression 32 along "a stable ridgeline,"
the soil "a yellow loess," wind lifting dust over

itself for whole ages into hills. Nothing here
        but earth and the grass catching the sky
to the earth in its million nets, they went down

into the dark, rose up in morning. I remember
        my grandfather's first school was a dug-out
below eastern Colorado plains before he graduated

to Denver where he took me past construction sites,
        machinery nesting in excavations,
intently arranging the future, the same time

I delighted in digging my grave in vacant lots
        of World War II, friends lobbing dirt grenades,
gargling explosions, or sitting alone, dreaming

inside my little shaft, almost buried in safety,
        hidden under the square bright sky.
Now at school in someone's deep empty home

several centuries too late, we look for evidence,
        labeling and sacking breakage, examining
the secondary chips of flint, the ransacked midden,

and finally reach—roof fallen, wall slumped—
        the floor worn firmly, before they moved,
by fifteen, twenty years of living, the river below

by day and corn by the river, each night the ridge
        with its companionable small fires.
I myself spent twenty years at home and left

for forty more, learning how long we travel
        in various companies, and slip away at night
from the sheer, vivid restlessness of our lives.

ANOTHER MEMENTO MORI

Hearing "September Song" in the background,
a woman's voice dark and smooth, I wonder
how many songs have been lost, hymns,
lullabies, love songs, in a confused hum.

"On Moonlight Bay—" mother and father sang
on trips in the V-8 Ford, both now transformed,
like the car, into various minerals.
Stole-my-heart, they warbled. Don't-go-way.

I wait for the last song at a funeral
because when it's over something's over
absolutely. If it didn't end,
no one would be dead, except that music
is required to stop at some point in order
to imitate life's overture, finale.

I know this one begins to end with precious-days
and dwindle-down and spend-with-you, but I
don't know the story, who these people are.
For a long time I didn't know the last line,
I went da-dum in my head to finish it
until a friend assured me it repeated

the line before, spend-with-you,
a doubled hopeful promise for an ending
which, oh-don't-go-way, I should have figured.

LIFE SCIENCES

I loved, for a couple of weeks, a girl
in high school biology class who moved
straight-backed with regal purity
across the room which shone with light

from the windows intricate with plants
blazing with photosynthesis, nature's first green
being gold, Frost wrote, as we had last year read
in a room above us on the second floor. One day

I finally spoke, how wonderfully she stood,
and stood hearing her softly explain
the metal rod pressed against her spine
and out to her shoulders holding her firmly.

Wordless, I retreated, not even knowing
I was starting the lessons of form, the iron
around our almost swooning bodies, a curve
of water in its supple vase, flesh in the poem,

song in its little cage. Along the bright windows
a half dozen aquaria bubbled, sighing like life,
grace and suffering breaking the surface.
Did you imagine, Ruth Meyer, I'd ever forget you?

GIRL AT THE RIVER

Something about the Ice Age catches my attention
        so I don't switch the channel. The Himalayas arose,
turning a stream of winds north, cooling the world an eon,

and to prove this today a young woman kneels
        beside a milky cascade, nothing around except
the rocks of the rest of Tibet. She is alone

and with the camera crew, I understand,
        though so American I constantly forget. "Carbon
dioxide," a narrator intones, the way it wears

from rocks into rivers calculating the rate of loss
        of something important. She slides a bottle sideways
into the continual rush, then caps and labels it

to assay later in camp. Though I have dabbled
        in the chilly music of variously tuned creeks,
this is brutally different, hard and remote, and I

am warm and old, ignorant of almost all
        the elements she measures. And I almost kneel
in the thin light of the screen, sadly prayerful

at the careless endurance of her momentary life,
        cold and rich like worn rock, like heavy-laden water
creamy with its suspensions, this girl gathering

the waters of her future, bending down again
        to the torrent, the cold ache of the gigantic past
streaming like science through her singular fingers.

OPEN SPACES

I sit down at the Vietnamese restaurant
accidentally facing the full-mirrored wall.

Two men at each of two other tables
sit with their backs to themselves

but I have only me, face-on, and I'm
amazed at how large the world is

behind me. I look at myself seriously.
I look serious. I begin to eat.

I am huge in the glass with my tiny plate
but I am small in the room where,

if it were a globe, I would be
about the size of Vietnam.

There are two rooms. I am in both.
There's no escaping me. Have I hauled

this huge emptiness around with me
all my life? Is this what the others saw

that I could not? Why they loved me
or why they didn't? When I leave,

I know what people passing me think:
so alone he seems, with that enormous

ache of air trailing along—behind him,
everything else in the world.

THE SCHOOL OF THE ART OF WINGS

As I drive past, a scatter of birds
    startles up from the field, the Vs
and Ws we children blackened in the sky—

blue paint above the always green fields
    or a mountain's pure purple triangle.
Every tree those years bore the circle

wound of a knothole for a home
    of something, hearts folded the same
on both sides, our handprints turned

into a turkey's tail, lessons for ways
    to see our world although no flower
in this present ditch is tulip or daisy,

our two favorite shapes of adorning
    gardens of houses smoking with welcome,
and, the letters of birds having left, I realize

only now we thought they were flying toward us
    over the fields, which are not green,
and coming home, nothing like what happens.

TAKE-OUT POINT

The young are throwing themselves off bridges
    this Sunday afternoon as my friend and I drift,
old men, around the bend—the river curling
    into shallows, depths, for only a moment all day—

to lurch aground as the skinny bomb of a boy
    streamlines feet first and splash, two girls
in tiny swimsuits by the sun-hot car leisurely
    murmuring their no doubt astonishing secrets.

We are aged enough they might think we were
    set adrift to die, if they thought of us,
so nonchalant toward the world
    they seem charmed, aloof, under a bridge

recording their names, years, all of us spending
    our lives, wasting them wonderfully
in the same direction. We stand around,
    pretending not to notice, then load canoe
as boy climbs into car with girls, gunning the way
    up hill toward home, river carrying
the salt of their sweet skin to some Atlantic
    as we drive gingerly into the next near future.

THE SINGING OF BOB AND CHARLENE

God, the Sunday radio suggests, is here,
      east of Cheyenne and Eden,
a landscape buzzing with lessons
      like Saul's disobedience who didn't
kill all the Ammonites he could.

Driving, I don't like this, but I listen,
      so I assume someone else
is listening and liking it, although
      only one house is in view,
then behind. The next song insists Jesus

is the friend of the weak, unlike
      his Father's feelings
toward the Ammonites, and then
      a host of stations surrounds me
with such promises and prayers

I switch into silence but when I pass
      precisely thirty-five Herefords
on a small rise I remember "He owns
      the cattle on a thousand hills"
sung Sunday nights at First Baptist

by Bob and red-headed Charlene Howe.
      I'm driving over an earth
the shape of air and water, a mild ravine
      some sacred course curved,
dry grass beautifully anonymous,

a landscape so familiar I think
      the same words each time
the way you can't say much more
      to someone than you love them,
and I could weep that this land

doesn't mind it's mostly forgotten,
        although they also sang
"His eye is on the sparrow," smiling,
        their faces bright as tears.
At the edge of Pine Bluffs I'm not sure

whether the all-white Mother
        of God, tall as a phone pole,
is in Wyoming or Nebraska
        but an empty freight comes
toward her, passes her by. After that,

the earth is infinite again, spare and large,
        as if the Old Testament
had been erased. "Mmm," we all nodded
        when Bob and Charlene finished,
and "A-men," someone mumbled.

Should I stay in Potter, Nebraska,
        the requisite forty days
and nights, I might know something
        about the unhowling wilderness
of my own mind, but I decide to drive

and next arrives a massive bluff
        someone has diminished
with crosses, then a ridge speared in its hump
        like a bison by the crossings of poles
for power, light, and talk, how great Thou art,

and "Mmm" we sighed when Bob
        and red-headed Charlene sat down,
their faces brimming with a holiness
        I didn't understand, except for the way,
God's eyes, I now brood over the face of the earth.

THE MOMENT OF SNOW

I remember snow each night that winter at the cabin
    in the Crazy Mountains, each morning
a kind of forgetfulness, a soft scatter over the grit
    of yesterday, wherever we'd worked or walked,

and I traced for years the way snow moves across Dakota,
    smokes on the highway, drifts in the ditch, but nothing
has stayed longer than one gray Colorado afternoon,
    7th grade, 8th, heads down in our usual ranks and files,

when a little hiss of notice rippled across the room
    and we looked up—one row at a time, it felt like—
at the sift of the fragile first flakes slanting down,
    carrying our dizzy eyes and hearts along.

Regularly irregular, it shuffled inside us,
    a relentless delicacy which might erase
everything we knew about our lives and teach us
    something else. I don't why that falling

still carries me down with it, or why,
    helpless, I've loved anything in my life. I do know
the shapes of houses fading, the trees
    dimming like twilight and how the multitude of snow
was an oblivion and nothing could save us,
    nor mother, nor father, the town to be buried
by steady uncertainties, the world coming loose,
    the first time something ceaseless had appeared

and we were beautiful enough to recognize it,
    who would never see each other again,
who would see each other the next day,
    who would no longer recognize ourselves.

NOT ABOUT CLOUDS

Let's say clouds are like books,
    each rich chapter rather like the last,
stratified on shelves along the horizon
    or curling in the cirrus of wispy thought,

or cumulus, those singular grand volumes,
    and on and on. All right, let's not.
But why do we wonder about
    those endlessly perishable generations?

"Alone I go to the white clouds and return,"
    Wang Wei wrote. And I read, after that,
the footnote of a scholar: "Simplicity,
    purity, harmony." In the mountains

of Colorado I watched come over the high pass
    each morning Purity, in the afternoon, Rain,
and have, for years now, lived beneath
    the sky coming apart, joining together,

like breathing. Tu Fu wrote he would follow the water
    that flows beyond the gate, "leaving behind
these white clouds," the average fifty thousand
    tons, I read, white being particularly heavy.

I think I'd prefer to die outside, lying on a hill,
    above me only sky and its lumbering travelers,
dying in a kind of evaporation since I'm in love
    still with the curved arrows of the water cycle

in grade school: high mountains, ocean, and
    in between those fluffy cartoons who gather up,
who let fall. Tu Fu has now left every one behind
    and Wang Wei is dead who yet lives

who is yet dead—where you stop
        thinking becomes your outlook—and I,
unlike him, am not getting any younger
        and have my own wine to drink.

Everything comes apart, everything joins.
        I must stop looking up so much.
Let's not say anything anymore. This is not
        about the clouds. Forget the clouds.

Part Two

MAN

FROM THE BOOK OF ROPE

First, there is love. Secondly,
the square knot, a perfect binding
of two equal loops, useful

for fastening gifts to each other
or, in the extreme, for closing bandages
over wounds, expected or not.

The sheetbend hooks unequal partners,
originally a rope to the twisted end
of a sail, something fastened against wind.

The bowline's loop won't close, good
for saving yourself in mountain-climbing,
or, in general, being lifted up, lowered.

Hitches bind us to things, thwarting
our drift, boat to a tree, horse to any rail—
two half-hitches, hundreds of half-hitches.

In the book of rope, three tests
for every knot: Is it easy to tie?
Will it stay tied firmly? And

finally, will it be easy to untie?
Which knots have we chosen?
What else sadly should we know?

IT WAS XENON, I THINK

                (Xe, number 54, atomic weight 131.30)

which someone used to illustrate
        our connections, how,
in one gulp of air, many

or few atoms we might inhale
        from Hitler's last breath,
or Christ's first, although we tend

to the horrible in such discussions,
        the same unreactive
bits getting around for millennia,

a point worth considering,
        another being how
chemicals combine, oxygen

changing its allegiances, carbon
        into who knows what,
so that I am a blend of the Atlantic,

tin, grass, a Mongol warrior, feldspar
        and you are bubblegum,
buffalo piss, ant, orchid, aluminum,

that both of us are rotting bone
        uniting to form us a kiss
with—xenos the neuter of stranger—all

these colorless little foreigners
        kissing in our mouths,
hardly ourselves, helpless, ignorant,

innocent, perpetual, the blood
        of people we don't know
hot in our hearts, running the world.

THE WHOLE TIME

In the hot different country
we drove one morning through
shattering yellow butterflies,

in the afternoon, black, little
shadows breaking around us.
We thought we were in a novel

but without the understandings
which develop in novels.
We came to a lake completely green

with a white house. We swam
and then we slept, dreaming colors.
We lost each other in cities

and found each other in cities.
We were always surprised.
The whole time we wrote down

what we ate so that later
we could ask, Do you remember?
and be able to answer, Of course.

It was so nice we took pictures
which we mailed to many people
we maybe didn't like that much.

Then we came home. There are colors
but not the same. There is, for example,
no yellow. Our history is thinner.

We don't sleep the same.
We remember getting lost
in black churches, found

in golden parks, and when
we woke up there
we always smiled and said

Here we are.
That is not the way
we wake up here.

MARRIAGE FIRE

When our marriage burned up
and then down, drifts of deception
under the doors almost smothering us
and ending with crackling anger
scorching whatever we'd papered over
until we both went aflame ourselves,

our friends came as clown-firemen,
scrambling out of a little red truck,
yelling and bumping into each other,
falling down with their big shoes in the air,
many dousing you with cool sympathy,
a few rolling me roughly in a blanket.

We should have had a smoke-alarm
or gone to counseling, they said,
and although some thought the vacant lot
looked better empty—our marriage
too big to begin with, too much
bright blue for the neighborhood—
most were angry it wasn't there
and since there was no second act
they jumbled back into their truck and left.

It was hard to sift through all that
darkness settling over the grounds.
You took half of the ashes. I took half.

PLAYING

One year it was bridge,
all Sunday, and one year
infidelity. You have to pay
attention to play bridge.
Things add up. Dummy,
my will wandered off.
The third year we tackled
backgammon. Someone was
the champion of each game.
I remember my weak defense,
how I shrugged off losses.

Now I've forgotten everything
about playing backgammon,
I realize, watching a boy
and girl in the coffee-house
set out the board, line themselves up,
and reach for the dice, rumbling
the dark cup to pour out
whatever will happen.

SHELF LIFE

Only now I discover the life span
        of spices, one to two years if ground—
the leafy herbs, a year or less. Farewell

to the faded brittle chervil my first marriage
        sprinkled into nothing, chives dried to grass,
parsley a summer I can't remember,

the dull grains of cayenne smoldering
        faithful, unfaithful, who would know?
These shelves are so familiar, a neighborhood

of jars neatly addressed behind their fences,
        I feel sad for our pride in assembling them,
wanting to do what we were supposed to.

I don't know why we cherished the coriander seeds,
        the coriander ground, what we promised ourselves
about the anise, expected of the cardamom.

We took the warnings so much to our hearts—
        the celery seed to be "used sparingly"
the bays "with much discretion"—we never ate

our possible omelets, concocted our Béarnaise sauce.
        On the edge of moving, I empty them out,
broadcasting the wishful ashes, foolishly

having taken usefulness daily for granted.
        What else have I not consumed? What else
not allowed to become even history?

SADNESSES

His sadness is a mile wide and an inch deep.
It hollows out banks beneath the edges of corn fields,
the stalks toppling like dazed obedient soldiers.

Her sadness is silver broken over rocks in sunlight,
cascading off granite cliffs, dashing itself into pieces.
She has become a national park of beautiful grief.

Their long sadness is the slow meeting of two rivers,
one closer to sky, the other to earth, the silt glinting
in their leisurely union. Nothing will ever be the same.

Hers is so slow he falls asleep watching it.
Theirs, it turns out, empties into another ocean.
His bores her with its obvious expectations.

Sometimes a sadness hides inside forests.
At other times, it becomes a public traffic.
Ours is surrounded by pleasant countryside.

We watched their sadness move out of sight
and still it came past, continuously.
We had never suspected this of them.

He wanted to use her sadness to leave
and her natural current allowed that.
He caught her sadness south like a leaf.

Theirs is so picturesque we build homes beside them,
draw off nourishment, refreshing ourselves at anniversaries.
Everyone's sadness is the deepest in North America.

Mine has disappeared into a field. One day I was sad,
the next I wasn't. Everything grew leaves around me, singing.
It was not eternal like sadness but yearly, like joy.

MARRIAGE TWO: A DAY AT THE BEACH

Not our honeymoon but near enough,
we lounged in rented chairs, the coast
of Florida so slowly sloping
that two girls a hundred yards out
were only up to their knees in sea,
the sun, since they had slipped off their tops,
down to their breasts, which I didn't call
to your attention, nor did I think
that unfaithful, lolling in a new
warm state, two blurred nymphs safely
cavorting afar, and I remember I squeezed
your hand in salute to our unknown future
and you squeezed back because I'd squeezed yours
because who knows what others think
like the two mermaids blinking through salt
toward shore—a grand fuzzy collection
of strangers with no lives to speak of—
who might think they could return to land
that way, breasts bare, hair weedy, walking
almost on water, sweeping their way
into Miami, toward their own double
wedding, perhaps at the Fontainebleau,
and although this doesn't happen I'm content
with how much we embrace of what seems
unreachable, eyes opening outward
or back from any vantage point,
hearing singing or not hearing singing.

DRIVING HOME, WHEREVER THAT IS

The red car behind me, small as a bright
drop of blood in the rear-view mirror,
grows larger and passes, a man driving,
a woman beside him, half-turned, one hand
casually propping her head, and listening.

The dark ridge of the Missouri valley
rises a few miles to the west, eons away,
"the longest division of geologic time
containing two or more eras."

If you were here, you'd be listening
as she was, if I were explaining "era"
comes from aera, a bronze Roman coin,
or something more personal, except that
now what's personal is you're not here.

In a wetland along the road, a duck
sits on the hump of a muskrat's den,
unconcerned, comic, at home and not,
perhaps putting together its winter plans
the way barn swallows are bunching
these mornings on the cool highways,
little radio signals sputtering in their blood.
In South Dakota, cattle clatter across
the highway to new pastures. In Wyoming
elk move on, antlered and knowledgeable.

It doesn't matter where home is. We obey
laws not knowing we obey, not knowing laws.
Winter edges down in the air of our bodies
and if not everything moves south toward you,
maybe I'm enough. Showing my eras,
I'm talking my way down river, Caesar
returning with stolen gold, with love.

ACCIDENTALS

I've bought a wrong book to read
at the sidewalk café, mistaking
one Takahashi for another,

Matsuo for Shinkichi, so it's
an accident. At the corner,
a taxi toots at a dozing car.

Shinkichi, who said once, as a cloud,
"I'm cheerful, whatever happens"
would not honk, but Matsuo, who writes

a man's tongue "teems with cruel ants,"
might honk viciously. As well: "Sleeping
is a ceaseless struggle with death"

which is not true for the woman who sleeps
back in our room, beautiful
even more because it's afternoon,

probably sweetly oblivious
even to that fire truck's blast
heading toward another accident.

Because I keep on reading the wrong book
while thinking of the right one
and because of everyone passing,

including that man who seems
a little too well pleased with himself,
because of what I was spared

when the fire truck did not turn my way,
because of a breeze I don't know,
stirring the curtains I imagine

around a woman composed
primarily of sunlight, I feel
not too well pleased with myself,

everything being an accident,
and not like a cheerful cloud
but, this afternoon, not damn far from it.

INSTRUCTIONS

Someone knows how to do everything.
I mean some one person knows how
to do some one thing, and draw
a diagram, such as making a bomb,

etc., but in this case to cut
flower stems with a knife
underwater, what this picture means.
I could be in Russia with these daffodils

and know to cut them underwater
with a knife. So someone knew that
and someone knows how to breed
varieties of daffodils. First, someone knows

there are different names. No,
one person knows one name apiece
so it takes a lot of them to run
the daffodil company, and one to know

it comes from the asphodel, showy flowers
akin to Narcissus—pseudonarcissus—
said to cover the Elysian Fields although
no one remembers that species. I run the water,

cut with a knife, someone else knowing
why water runs, knives cut, only you knowing
what you'll think of them when you arrive
down our street called for someone else

and home into the marriage we've made,
both of us, in this case, knowing it, following
the instructions we momentarily concoct,
giving it whole varieties of beautiful names.

DINING ALONE WITH EVERYONE

I'm sitting in The French Cafe
in Omaha, large photos around
of people sitting in a French cafe
in France, no doubt, shadows now
of shadows, and I'm sipping
the house cabernet, thinking
of you in another city and suddenly
feel the heavy thrill of loving
swell in the ruby globe of my chest.

At the next table a white-haired woman
in black nods to another some knowledge
worth a wrinkle of concern; behind them two men
in business suits are pleased with business,
and I'm exquisitely concerned with my own life.

My mother thought a train station
profound, all those different lives
moving on, she'd murmur, not unlike,
from our mountain walk, the small waterfall
which, she reminded me later, even if
we forgot was still pouring down
which I thus never have forgotten.

The waiter places the silverware,
tenderly personal, before me, my napkin
folded as intricately as Notre Dame.
I love you and Paris, all of us—even
that darkened water plunging relentlessly
over itself, out of our attention.

LOVE ALONG THE RIVER

There are plenty of the usual discussions
        inside the river today, incessant
miniature arguments along the bank.
        The world looks always
in some sort of general agreement

but I'm not sure. Is there only one song?
        Yes, say the multiple clouds. No,
say the cottonwoods in their single upright
        wisdom, leaves fluttering
a mass of minor variations.

On the river, we glide a current smooth
        as the shore though thick swells constantly
bubble up from irregularities at the bottom,
        lift and collapse consistently at our side
as accompaniment, something we carry,

although, once grounded, we watch them
        glide past in the current we recently were.
At night one cottonwood log becomes
        a multitude of flaming rooms, windows
opening and closing. We don't know

if we love our similarities
        or our contrasts more—we will
never know—and we begin to sleep.
        River moves on, inhumanly, all night,
the easiest way. We wake

at the same time, our dreams different, or so
        we tell each other by the water,
the silver river that looks like dawn
        the way at midnight it looked like midnight.

Part Three

LAUGHING

WHAT IT'S LIKE NOW

All my first young loves are now
old women. Well. One by one

they write to me. I'm getting
smaller, they say. Please forget.

And I do note lately how the stars
seem more precious, how the bean fields

nearing harvest lie more supple
with their encapsulated secrets, although

I thought old men would know more
about earth or love or mornings than I do,

standing at sunrise in my own backyard,
married for years, dazzled by my ignorance.

NAMING NAMES

I love the words of the name red winged black bird
though my philosopher daughter tells me descriptions
are not real names. And oh I know how the words fail,

turning bright blue prairie blossoms to Spiderwort
a farmer calls Cow Slobber. And I know how lazy
and local we get, talking of buffalo berry, buffalo bird,

buffalo grass, Indian grass or fig. Someone called it
Indian bean, the broad catalpa, a tree I met in Kansas
as a child, that place that means the wind, wind people,
south-wind people, a tree whose sound meant flowers,

"head with wings," in the round mouths of the Creek,
a tree which is Bignonia, imagine, in New Latin, when

we wanted to be neutral as science and hence named
a tree for the Abbe Bignon, New Latin librarian
to Louis XIV, hence honoring air again. "Te amo"

my 8th grade girlfriend's friends dared Jayne to say
which didn't mean she loved me, since it was
another language. Later, I took Latin and by now

Miss Hixon's joined Marcus Aurelius who joined,
as he knew he would, three men he names
as learning from and of whom, a footnote says,

"nothing is known" and who, anyway, wrote in Greek
or, for all we know, water. Or the air. Might as well
be air, I've thought, language only a shape of lips.

In Mabel Hixon's Latin class, Gene sat heavily
beside me in his stained work-clothes, his face
a laborious puzzle over the text, the rest of us

wondering why he read, why he was even there.
At our 40th reunion, he turned out to own
the county's biggest truck farm, thank you,

planting food in Latin—a union of onions,
the radical roots of the radish—and other tongues,
tomat, batata, the ancient bha-bha of the bean,

the grains of corn gardeners first called maize,
and the people ate the names and they were good.
It doesn't matter we give every wind a name

that dies, Mabel and Marcus other people now.
This breathing sound is how we call, our only ways
to say te amo to the air and bring it back again,

te amo to the black bird with its red spot wing,
te amo tomato and rosy wort, and green grass grown
and Gene and Jayne and all the, all the names.

LISTENING IN SUMMER

Now glory be to good
things singing around us
in the darkness, listen.

Inside the crickets'
scalloped chirping, scrapers
trilling against dry files,

the grasshoppers rasping
from their stalks, the sticks
and thin strings of katydids,

cicadas drumming thickly
in the thick trees vanishing
into the throbbing dark,

we listen until we're not
listening. Our ears fizz
with their electric persistence.

We do not care insects see-saw
in the hazardous guessings of sex,
or that cicadas have churned

for years under the earth, or
that in a dark, large world
they are leagues apart, singing

to find each other, themselves.
The world is all alive
is all we know, something

thrilling the air, a murmur
reminding us of every
summer we remember,

something awake all night
which numbs, soothing us under.
Sleeping, our bodies cool

Only the crickets insist.
Is it? Is it? they ask all night
and answer, It is. It is.

ONE OF THOSE DAYS

Each day I am in love
with something, in full
wonder at what's given.
Yesterday, it was partly
some sparkling Mozart
but mostly, five minutes
earlier, the announcer's remark:
"Mozart's coming up
in five minutes."

Today it's the beginning
of a sentence in a book
about Tu Fu—"In the spring
of 761..." regarding several
short songs, an ancient fresh breath.

I realize the museum next door
is chock-full of bones and the perpetual
birthdays of rock, that millennia
shift only a few pebbles, and that mostly
everything is utterly forgotten
but I'm enthralled with the spring
of 761, hold it in my arms all night.

Although Mozart dies young
and Tu Fu's hopes turn out false
always, I can't resist singing to myself
the knowledge of unknowable springs,
musical as arpeggios of cherry,
those immortal blossoms, and, above,
those particular clouds passing away.

ABOUT EIGHT MINUTES OF LIGHT
IN THE MEADOW

I'm lying in tall grass, half dazed, watching
a fly on the bright opposite side of a leaf,
its dark hairy silhouette emblazoned
by a sun 93 million miles away.
By the time I remember this, the fly's gone.

At the meadow's edge, a dead pine
has stayed caught in its fall by another pine,
branches entangled, the last three years
at least. Anything looked at long enough
becomes perfect. Three years is long enough.

Two dark soft fir stand across the meadow
from each other and this afternoon, this
moment, a small bird crosses from one
and lands in the other, sparks of singing
glittering in the middle of the air.

A butterfly passes, waggles away,
folds its wings thinly up and
disappears, a small door closing.
I wonder how many thousand others
are just now invisible in this meadow

where I am dazzled with marvel—
illumination after simply illumination.
At the speed of light, this sun's shine
is about eight minutes old, though all's
always in this new time. And now this one.

COMPARISONS

In the middle of a river, I listen
to the businessman comparing business
to an orchestra, each instrument

properly contributing,
each part a part of the whole.
The orchestra, however,

compares itself to a river—
flutes of light, cellos bubbling along
in the push and flow

of adagio, crescendo,
allegro—in rushes and deep swirling.
But this current river

compares itself placidly
to a business, all its appropriate
liquid departments

working in unison
toward singular goals, closing up shop
here, opening there,

reorganizing itself now
through a downturn of driftwood,
so the two of us stop

humming our various tunes
and backpaddle furiously in order
not to go bankrupt, get flat, or wet.

GOODNIGHTS

The children are out tonight, blinking at fireflies
dragging their small illuminations as they lumber
slowly upward through thick air. Two thousand species

in the world and in this backyard it's pyralis, common
east of the Rockies, who flare each six or seven seconds,
and it's the children who, every ten seconds or so,

bring one up to us for inspection, their palms
reflecting the yellowish glow of Lampyridae,
the family of the Shining Fire.

We are at home, though we're not quite sure
of the night since it seems something fragile
is taking a lovely direction, an aimless dancing,

but it's air rubbing the luciferin in their plump bodies
so they become little lit princes of the darkness
with the princesses waiting flightless in the grass

and watching since these are signals for sex, a code
embodied in their ons and offs. For everything's
a signal, it's just that we don't often understand,

the butterfly's design, the drop of temperature caught
on the breeze that signifies something we don't hear,
the night pulsing around us with foreign interpretations,

because the world's not written in our language,
children. You see by now that what we catch these nights—
which, anyway, was not meant for us—we soon let go.

And listen—the wormy larvae glow a year or two
before they grow to beetles flashing patterns heavy
with desire. These are the adults. They last a month.

So say goodnights now, and to everything,
to each one give a good night's kiss, and sleep
away in rise and fall, the very breath of darkness.

ON MUSIC

I am driving the Interstate listening to,
of all things, a Strauss waltz. Outside,
they are cutting the grass along the roadway.
We think we have escaped from everything.

The last piece I heard the woman,
who died of cancer in two years, play
on the piano was Clair de Lune.
Clair de Lune, for Christ's sake.
For Christ's sake, cancer.

A boy I knew who played trombone
in high school died of a heart attack
at 50, they told me at the reunion,
and all I could think was that
a trombone player had died.

Johann, known as the Younger,
Strauss, I'm told afterward, wrote
"more than three hundred waltzes"
and died in 1899, the year my grandfather
got married, who later sang one line
from the cowboy "On the Navajo Trail,"
each morning for every day in his long life.

"Well, whaddya know?" he'd sing
and grin. "It's morning already."
No one owns that grass, this road, the air.
Yes, we do. ONE, two three. Yes, we do.

AT A TABLE ON SUTTER & LEAVENWORTH

From the city bus, locals look out
at me, a tourist. They look like tourists
on buses looking out at a local.

A girl carries a water bottle by the neck.
Each year we have new baggage.

I wouldn't want a black leather jacket,
it's too warm, although it may get cold
in which case that man carrying one will be right.

"That's terrible," the guy two tables up
says twice, but it doesn't sound like he means it.

A surprise: an Asian girl brisks up the street
in an almost skin-colored top, breasts bouncing.
Is she nude? No. Is she Asian? Is there a street?

The sun shines on parked cars
the way it shines on granite in the mountains.

I wish I had a blue silk scarf to wear
around my neck, like this woman, slender,
sliding by. It would change my life.

Another bus goes by and no one
notices, not even the passengers.

It is as easy for that gray pigeon to fly
as it is to be on the sidewalk.
It may even be easier, but here we are.

A black pigeon with orange feet, a tiny
customs inspector, nods I'm free to go.

Down the walk, past gum-foil and papers,
on top of a trash can, a gathering
of dried zinnias. Some gift?

In a crack between sidewalk and wall,
a weed is ready to blossom after I'm gone.

APPEARANCES

Some of us seem ready for battle
like the young man passing by
in fatigues, a mimic of motley shadows
and sun, although distinctive enough
against the Hallmark shop across the street.

I'm wearing jeans, dress shirt, tweed jacket
so I may be a professor of English,
a discovery which could depress me
the way it depresses me when my students
say some story depresses them,
assuming I actually have students.

Maybe someone stole my cowboy outfit
and left me this one. I remember
a football uniform in junior high
in which I felt deliciously constrained,
felt stronger, faster, though I wasn't.
And I once wore a jacket with leather
elbow patches promising my life
would be spent with elbows on a desk,
perhaps assembling automatic weapons.

That grandmother has a sweater
showing she owns a Swiss chalet.
That man's hat should be festooned
with fishhooks but it's not, suggesting
he's a fisherman with a new hat.
Although these may be costumes
hastily borrowed from back stages
and then in the footlights forgotten,
we appear completely pleased
with how we've dressed ourselves.

Now I discover, consulting my watch,
which I don't remember, I must leave
to go to a desk of some sort but who knows
what will be there? Who knows the terrible
or trivial work I am suited for? Watch me
disappear down the walk, someone
you may later have to describe to police
as, if necessary, I'm ready to do for you.

RISING UP TOGETHER

At the art museum, doors open into the room
of the elevator, a half dozen people
idly looking up to see who's coming in, and

I've just been visiting a doctor who, after months,
has told me there's no longer cancer under my skin
so there's "no need to meet again" (somewhat

the relief and reluctance of tired lovers parting,
only beginning to understand their freedom) and,
before the appointment, drinking a compliment of coffee

in the motel room, surprised the Comedy Channel
was on at 7:30, night-time laughter harsh so early
in the morning while I waited for a doctor's routine,

sunken in myself, and pushed through 45 channels,
re-runs and late-breaking news spliced together,
to then walk the collage of the Minneapolis streets,

phone poles plastered with flyers inviting me
to concerts that had already happened
or asking about lost pets, and the ragged spaces

where flyers had been ripped away, the old wood bristling
with a contagion of staples, and multiple alleys
spray-painted with sweeping, day-glo warnings

that "Life is" a number of things, none of them
entirely pleasant, and to climb the doctor's stairs
and then, after his welcome back goodbye, to enter

the museum to see Marc's "Large Blue Horses" which
they certainly are, poised in their dream of a meadow,
and stand by the real counter of Segal's "Diner,"

unfrozen myself now, by the white plaster customer
with head down, studying today's real empty cup
while the plaster waitress waits forever for coffee

to come from the gleaming urn, and finally Horsfield's
huge black/white photograph of a Krakow jazz club
twenty years ago, which is completely the art

of accident, the figures composing themselves
in an instant's flash as a man and woman dancing,
her face exuberant although looking off to the left,

his guessed at since we see only the back of his head,
and in the grainy background a man in a white shirt
clapping, his hands apart for just that moment

of silence before everything continues,
and the woman will turn finally back
to her partner and perhaps we even see his face

turned, smiling, as I smile at my new friends as if I
had been waiting a long time and step inside,
the doors closing like two large hands in applause,

in prayer, and join everyone else, all of us
in the elevator's home rising upward together,
together at last, at last and alive.

LOSS

Though I have lost mother, some memory,
        a camera with film, dark pieces of Oregon inside,
numerous coins, pens, points—there is no loss.

Although the violin disintegrates in the swamp
        and the cobbled path to the Mayan cenote
is missing a few round notes, there is no loss.

It seems there is loss because I know nothing more
        of Judy whom I half-loved, or a favorite teacher
who is dead, or the umbrella I left in Portugal

but there is no loss because my teacher's
        loved comedian in the '50s, George Gobel,
is also dead, and because Judy surely has lost

an umbrella at least once in her life. It feels
        like loss, those opposite landscapes of film
I'll never recognize, and it feels like loss,

the photographs I can't name the place of
        or am dumb about the year, and here
is one I know: the title of the ornate church,

even the date of that blue sunshine,
        though not the woman in a red scarf
moving away at the left, head lowered.

But Judy, this is the amazing thing,
        walks this moment in a city—
moving away to the left and it's not raining—

neither thinking of loss nor certainly of me,
    looking forward to something small
which makes her smile and then, further amused

to realize she is smiling, smile more
    and no one around her notices
this moment and nothing is ever lost.

FALTERING

It's the way you laugh at your own
        minor frailty when no one
is around. Being old helps.

Being alone helps. Last year
        I followed a trail up a ravine
that became a path, became
        a faint track deer had rarely used,
that became a nest of willows
        and tall entangling grass
I was finally crawling through,
        so ridiculous, at last,
I had to roll over and laugh.

Today, I stumbled over stones
        by the river, each foot trying
to rectify the fault of the last
        and failing, I like a lunatic
staggering over rocks but not
        falling, worthy of a smile.

This is human. It could be
        merely a dust of snow shaken
out of a tree in your face
        reminding you that in this world
you're often prey to whatever
        it is you're under. Animal is
something else. When I was child
        our plush cat miscalculated
a leap from couch to shelf, pretending
        huffily that nothing had happened

and the other day a squirrel
        in our backyard slipped up to slip off
the fence, claws scratching all the way down
        to land, and then promptly forgot.

And isn't that our glory? Sprawled
        in the mud, tripped up by a log,
half-in the river, bemused
        by nature temporarily
until we're bemused forever.
        What's not to love? Snow in our faces,
we shrug, shake our great heads, and grin.
        Especially old, especially alone,
I laugh as, walking, I falter.